from SEA TO SHINING SEA

KENTUCKY

By Dennis Brindell Fradin

CONSULTANTS

James C. Klotter, Ph.D., State Historian and Director,
Kentucky Historical Society

Robert L. Hillerich, Ph.D., Professor Emeritus, Bowling Green State University;
Consultant, Pinellas County Schools, Florida

CHILDRENS PRESS®
CHICAGO

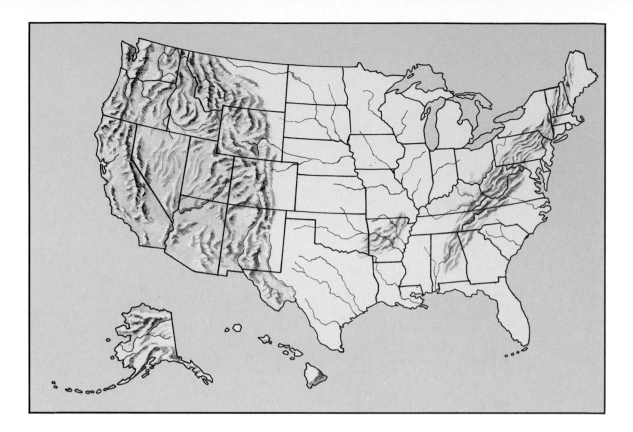

Kentucky is one of the fourteen states in the region called the South. The other southern states are Alabama, Arkansas, Delaware, Florida, Georgia, Louisiana, Maryland, Mississippi, North Carolina, South Carolina, Tennessee, Virginia, and West Virginia.

For my uncle, Bernard Brindel, with love

Front cover picture: Whitehaven, the State of Kentucky Welcome Center, in Paducah; page 1: Kentucky Horse Park, Lexington; back cover: Natural Arch, Daniel Boone National Forest

Project Editor: Joan Downing
Design Director: Karen Kohn
Research Assistant: Judith Bloom Fradin
Typesetting: Graphic Connections, Inc.
Engraving: Liberty Photoengraving

THIRD PRINTING, 1994.

Library of Congress Cataloging-in-Publication Data

Fradin, Dennis B.
  Kentucky / by Dennis Brindell Fradin.
    p.   cm. — (From sea to shining sea)
  Includes index.
  Summary: An overview of the Bluegrass State,
introducing its history, geography, industries, sites of
interest, and famous people.
  ISBN 0-516-03817-6
  1. Kentucky—Juvenile literature. [1. Kentucky.]
I. Title. II. Series: Fradin, Dennis B. From sea to shining
sea.
F451.3.F7   1993   92-38810
976.9—dc20   CIP
                                                AC

Table of Contents

Keeneland Race Course, near Lexington

INTRODUCING THE BLUEGRASS STATE

Kentucky is in the southeastern United States. The name *Kentucky* comes from the Indian word *Ken-tah-teh*. Some say it means the "land where we will live." Another possible meaning is "meadowland." Kentucky is nicknamed the "Bluegrass State." Part of the state is covered with bluegrass. This lovely grass has blue-green leaves.

Bourbon is an alcoholic drink.

Kentucky is rich in racehorses, coal, tobacco, and bourbon. Each spring, Louisville hosts the Kentucky Derby. That is the country's most famous horse race. Kentucky is also rich in its history. Daniel Boone helped settle Kentucky in the 1770s. Abraham Lincoln and Jefferson Davis were both born in Kentucky. They led the opposing sides during the Civil War (1861-1865).

The Bluegrass State is special in other ways. Where does the United States keep most of its gold? Where is the world's longest known cave system? Where were boxer Muhammad Ali and singer Loretta Lynn born? The answer to these questions is: Kentucky!

Overleaf: Cumberland Gap National Historic Park

A picture map of Kentucky

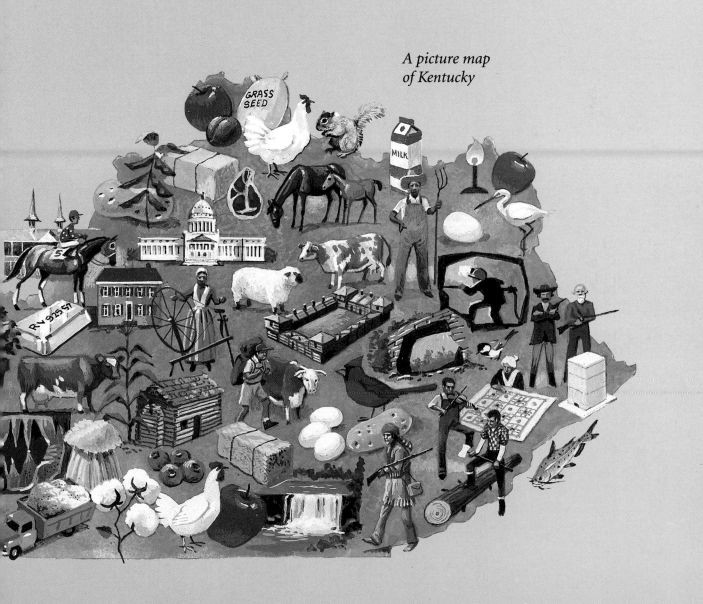

"Heaven Is a Kentucky of a Place"

"Heaven Is a Kentucky of a Place"

"Heaven is a Kentucky of a place," a minister said long ago. Today, Kentucky still has lovely woodlands, farms, and mountains. The Bluegrass State is heavenly but small. Kentucky covers 40,395 square miles. Only thirteen of the other forty-nine states are smaller.

Kentucky is in the part of the country called the South. Seven states border Kentucky. Ohio, Indiana, and Illinois are to the north. Missouri lies to the west. Tennessee is Kentucky's neighbor to the south. Virginia and West Virginia are to the east.

Geography

Kentucky has five different land regions: the Appalachian Mountains, the Bluegrass, the Pennyroyal, the Western Coal Field, and the Jackson Purchase.

The Appalachian Mountains are in eastern Kentucky. These mountains have much of Kentucky's coal. Black Mountain is in southeast Kentucky. It stands 4,145 feet above sea level. It is the state's highest point.

Autumn trees in the Red River Gorge Geological Area, eastern Kentucky

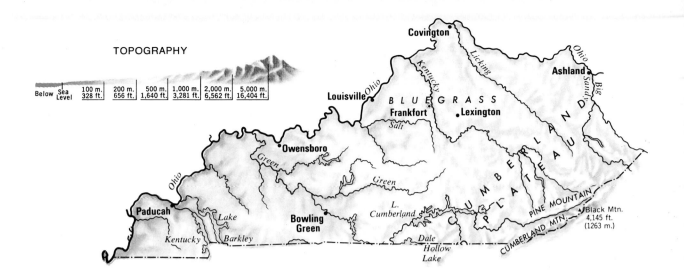

TOPOGRAPHY

Below Sea Level | 100 m. 328 ft. | 200 m. 656 ft. | 500 m. 1,640 ft. | 1,000 m. 3,281 ft. | 2,000 m. 6,562 ft. | 5,000 m. 16,404 ft.

Covington

Ashland

Ohio

Big Sandy

Louisville

B L U E G R A S S

Frankfort

Lexington

Licking

Kentucky

Ohio

Salt

Owensboro

Green

Green

C U M B E R L A N D   P L A T E A U

Paducah

Lake

Kentucky

Barkley

Bowling Green

L. Cumberland

PINE MOUNTAIN

CUMBERLAND MTN.

Black Mtn. 4,145 ft. (1263 m.)

Dale Hollow Lake

The Bluegrass region is in north-central Kentucky. This rolling land is famous for its horse farms. Corn and tobacco are grown there. Kentucky's biggest cities, Louisville and Lexington, are in the Bluegrass. The Pennyroyal region takes up much of south-central and southwestern Kentucky. A mint called pennyroyal grows on this land. Rich farmland covers the Pennyroyal. Beneath the Pennyroyal are many caves. Mammoth Cave is the most famous one.

The Western Coal Field and Jackson Purchase are in western Kentucky. The Western Coal Field lies in the northwest. It is a hilly area that is rich in coal and farmland. The Jackson Purchase makes up Kentucky's western tip. This land includes swamps and other lowlands. Kentucky's lowest point is here, along the Mississippi River. It is only 257 feet above sea level.

It is called the Jackson Purchase because General Andrew Jackson helped the United States buy the land from the Indians in 1818.

9

Mountain laurel shrubs (above) and other wildflowers (below) brighten Kentucky during the spring.

WATERS, WOODS, AND WILDLIFE

Four rivers form much of Kentucky's borders. The Mississippi River flows along its western border. The Ohio River forms Kentucky's northern border. The Big Sandy and Tug Fork rivers curve along its eastern border. The Cumberland River starts and ends in Kentucky. It winds mainly through Tennessee, however. The Kentucky River is 260 miles long. It flows completely inside the Bluegrass State. The Green is another major river that twists through Kentucky.

Most of Kentucky's large lakes were made by building dams on rivers. Kentucky Lake covers 250 square miles. It is one of the world's largest artificially made lakes.

About half of Kentucky is covered by forest. The Kentucky coffeetree is the state tree. Coffee doesn't really grow on it. Pioneers made a drink from the tree's seeds. It tasted like coffee. Pine, cedar, ash, hickory, oak, maple, and walnut trees also grow there.

Wildflowers add color to Kentucky's meadows and mountainsides. Goldenrod is the state flower. Azaleas, violets, and buttercups abound.

Kentucky's huge forestlands, many rivers, and colorful wildflowers beautify the state, especially during the spring and fall months.

Above left and opposite page, top: Raccoons and foxes such as these are among the animals that live in Kentucky. Above right: Late summer in the Berea area countryside

Deer, raccoons, foxes, squirrels, opossums, and rabbits live in Kentucky's forests. A few bobcats roam through the mountains. Bats live in Kentucky's many caves. The Kentucky cardinal is the state bird. The Kentucky River is a good place to see great blue herons. Catfish, bluegills, trout, and walleye swim in Kentucky's waters.

CLIMATE

The Bluegrass State enjoys a warm to moderate climate. Summer temperatures over 80 degrees

Fahrenheit are common. The state can get much hotter than that. Greensburg set Kentucky's record high temperature. It reached 114 degrees Fahrenheit there on July 28, 1930.

Winters are generally mild in Kentucky. Louisville's January temperatures often reach about 45 degrees Fahrenheit. Yet, now and then, it gets very cold in Kentucky. Cynthiana set the state's record low temperature. It dropped to minus 34 degrees Fahrenheit on January 28, 1963. About 15 inches of snow fall each year on Kentucky.

Below: Winter in Powell County

From Ancient Times Until Today

FROM ANCIENT TIMES UNTIL TODAY

About 300 million years ago, much of Kentucky was swampy. Plants grew in the swampland. When they died, a thick layer of plant material formed. Over the ages, this turned into coal.

Long ago, huge beavers lived in Kentucky. Mastodons and mammoths lived there, too. Big Bone Lick in northern Kentucky is a mastodon and mammoth graveyard. Those animals became stuck in the mud and died there.

Opposite: The Water House at Shaker Village

AMERICAN INDIANS

Ancient Indians reached Kentucky about 15,000 years ago. Those early Indians lived in caves and along cliffs. Tools several thousand years old have been found at Mammoth Cave.

Later Indian groups in Kentucky included the Cherokee, Shawnee, Chickasaw, and Delaware. Kentucky's Indians built their homes with wood and bark. They grew corn, squash, and beans. The Indians hunted deer in the woods. They caught fish and turtles along the streams.

This shell pendant was uncovered in Kentucky. It shows a man using a stone like those used in a hoop-and-stick game played by many southeastern American Indians.

When settlers crossed into Kentucky through the Cumberland Gap, they began to discover beautiful areas like the river gorge of the Big South Fork of the Cumberland (above).

EXPLORERS AND SETTLERS

England founded the Virginia colony in 1607. This was the first of England's thirteen American colonies. English explorers entered Kentucky from Virginia. Abraham Wood sent agents in 1654. Gabriel Arthur came in 1673.

By 1750, the American colonists were feeling crowded. They began thinking about moving west to Kentucky. There was a problem though. Mountains blocked the way like a giant wall.

In 1750, Thomas Walker discovered a mountain pass. This pass was named the Cumberland Gap. Kentucky, Virginia, and Tennessee meet there. Daniel Boone of North Carolina followed this pass into Kentucky. He hunted in Kentucky between 1767 and 1773.

Early in 1775, Boone blazed the Wilderness Road through the Cumberland Gap. This trail led westward to central Kentucky. Boone built Boonesboro where the trail ended. Later in 1775, he brought his family and other settlers to Kentucky. They lived at Boonesboro, on the Kentucky River.

James Harrod beat Boone in building Kentucky's first pioneer town, though. Harrod led

settlers into Kentucky from Pennsylvania in 1774. That June they founded Harrodsburg.

STATEHOOD AND GROWTH

Until 1776, Kentucky was part of the Virginia colony. After 1776, Kentucky was part of the state of Virginia. In that year, the Americans broke from England. They fought and won the Revolutionary War (1775-1783). The Americans then formed a new country. It was called the United States of America.

In the 1780s, Americans poured into Kentucky. They came by land over the Wilderness Road. They

Kentucky's first two settlements have been reconstructed. Fort Boonesborough (above) is near Boonesboro. Old Fort Harrod (below) is in Harrodsburg.

came by flatboat along the Ohio River. Once in Kentucky, the pioneers built log cabins and planted crops. Louisville, Lexington, and Frankfort were founded. By 1790, Kentucky had almost 75,000 people. That was enough people for statehood.

On June 1, 1792, Kentucky became the fifteenth state. It was the second one after Vermont to join the original thirteen. Lexington was the first state capital. Frankfort became the capital in 1793.

The new state grew fast. Kentucky's population rose from 73,677 in 1790 to 779,828 in 1840. New settlers kept arriving. Large families added to the population. For example, Jefferson Davis was

The Old State Capitol, in Frankfort

the youngest of ten children. Davis later became a political leader.

Pioneer Kentuckians made candles and soap. Pioneer women made clothes for their families. They colored them with dye made from marigold flowers and onion skins. Women also gathered to make quilts. These get-togethers were called quilting bees. Pioneer children played with homemade apple-head dolls.

Kentucky became known for certain products. By 1839, Kentucky was the leading hemp-growing state. Fibers from this plant were used to make rope. By 1839, Kentucky also led at raising horses, tobacco, corn, and rye. Kentuckians also made a kind of whiskey. It was called bourbon, for Kentucky's Bourbon County. They used some of their corn and rye for this drink.

In the 1800s, hemp (above) was a big Kentucky crop. Pioneer Kentuckians spun and dyed their own yarn (below).

SLAVERY AND THE CIVIL WAR

Kentucky and the rest of the South allowed slavery. Black slaves worked in Kentucky's hemp and tobacco fields. By the 1830s, one-fourth of all Kentuckians were black slaves.

The northern states had outlawed slavery. Nearly all white southerners wanted to keep slavery.

A Republican campaign banner for 1860

White Kentuckians, however, were divided about slavery. James Birney and Cassius Marcellus Clay were against slavery. In 1840 and 1844, Birney ran for president but lost. Clay founded an antislavery newspaper in 1845. It was called the *True American*. Because of his views, Clay made many enemies. He had to guard his home with a cannon!

Kentucky-born Abraham Lincoln was also against slavery. He didn't want slavery to be allowed in the new western lands. Lincoln ran for president in 1860. He won and became the sixteenth president.

White southerners feared that Lincoln would end slavery in the South. The southern states began seceding from (leaving) the United States in December 1860. They formed the Confederate States of America. Jefferson Davis became president of the Confederacy.

In 1861, the Civil War began. It was fought between the Confederacy (the South) and the Union (the North). Both sides wanted Kentucky to join them. The state officially sided with the Union. But a group also set up a Confederate Kentucky government. Kentucky had a star in both flags—Confederate and Union. Kentucky families had sons who faced each other in battle. Former Kentucky

governor John J. Crittenden's two sons were opposing Civil War generals.

Three big Civil War battles were fought in Kentucky in 1862. The Union won the Battle of Mill Springs. The Confederates won the Battle of Richmond. Kentucky's bloodiest Civil War battle had no clear-cut winner. This was the Battle of Perryville. It was fought on October 8, 1862. About 7,500 soldiers were killed or wounded at Perryville.

The Union won the war in April 1865. In that year, the United States government ended slavery throughout the country.

A replica of Abraham Lincoln's boyhood home near Hodgenville

Kentucky's Union soldiers included nearly 25,000 black men.

Tobacco farming became important in Kentucky in the late 1800s.

TOBACCO, COAL, AND WORLD WARS

Hemp lost importance in the late 1800s. Instead, tobacco farming boomed in the Bluegrass State. Kentucky was the leading tobacco-growing state from 1865 to 1929. By 1904, a few tobacco companies set the price of tobacco. Farmers did not make much money. Kentucky's western farmers fought these companies in the Black Patch War (1904-1909). From this war came the tobacco auctions. At the auctions, tobacco is purchased through open bidding.

In the early 1900s, Kentucky became a great coal-mining state. Coal provided heat and fuel for American homes, steel mills, and factories. But coal miners led very hard lives. Mine accidents killed or crippled many workers. Miners became sick from breathing coal dust. Mining families usually lived in towns owned by the mining companies. Prices might be high in these company towns. Often the housing was poor.

In 1917, the United States entered World War I (1914-1918). About 80,000 Kentuckians in uniform helped win this war. Kentuckian Samuel Woodfill single-handedly knocked out five enemy machine-gun nests. American Expeditionary Forces (AEF) General John J. Pershing called him the outstanding figure of the war.

Coal mining boomed. Coal was needed to fuel the country's factories. The factories made weapons for the war.

In the 1920s, the coal boom ended. Miners lost their jobs. Others had their pay cut. The miners banded together to fight for better conditions. The United Mine Workers of America helped. This is a labor union. There were fights between union miners and the mining companies. Dozens of Kentuckians died in the shootings and bombings. Much of the fighting took place in Harlan County. In 1931, it was called "Bloody Harlan County." In 1938, the miners won higher pay and safer working conditions.

In the early 1900s, Kentucky coal miners led very hard lives.

The coal miners' fight took place during the Great Depression (1929-1939). This was a time of hardship for the whole country. Many Kentucky families lost their farms. Franklin D. Roosevelt (FDR) was elected president in 1932. FDR started the New Deal. It created jobs for many people.

New Deal projects in Kentucky included school construction and adult-education programs. The Tennessee Valley Authority (TVA) began. Flooding of the Tennessee and Cumberland rivers was stopped through the TVA. In 1936, the United States started storing its gold at Fort Knox. Many Kentuckians got jobs at the fort.

World War II (1939-1945) helped end the Great Depression. Kentuckians got jobs making rubber, jeeps, and airplane parts. About 325,000 Kentucky men and women served their country in the armed forces.

CHANGES, GROWTH, AND CHALLENGES

Kentucky underwent great changes during the 1950s and 1960s. Across America, blacks were still treated unfairly. Particularly in the South, black children were not allowed to attend schools with white children. Blacks couldn't enter the same hotels or

The United States stores its gold at Fort Knox (above).

public bathrooms as whites. This racial segregation occurred throughout the South.

In 1954, the United States Supreme Court ruled that schools must be integrated. Black children and white children were to attend the same schools. Under Governors Lawrence W. Wetherby and Albert B. "Happy" Chandler, Kentucky integrated its schools peacefully. Other southern states fought school integration.

In 1966, Kentucky adopted a Civil Rights Act. It guaranteed black Kentuckians their rights as citizens. Kentucky was the first southern state to have such a civil-rights law.

Governors Chandler (above) and Wetherby helped Kentucky integrate its schools peacefully (below).

A Parade of Breeds at Kentucky Horse Park

A big vacationland opened in west Kentucky in 1963. This was the Land Between the Lakes. In 1978, the Kentucky Horse Park opened in Lexington. These two places brought many visitors to Kentucky. By 1980, tourism was a huge business.

In the 1970s, the United States suffered a fuel shortage. The demand for Kentucky coal grew. But the coal-mining boom had a bad side. Nearly half the state's coal comes from strip mining. This involves tearing the ground away to get the coal. Strip mining causes soil loss and water pollution. In

1977, the United States Congress passed a law. It limited the damage from strip mining. Mine owners must restore stripped land when they are through with a mine. They must fill in the land and plant trees.

Manufacturing was also growing in Kentucky. In 1988, Toyota opened its first plant in the United States. This was in Georgetown, Kentucky. Nearly eighty car-parts plants opened in Kentucky by 1989.

Kentucky celebrated its 200th birthday on June 1, 1992. Kentucky began its third century of statehood with problems, however. The Bluegrass State remains one of the poorest states. The average income in the United States was about $24,000 per worker in 1990. Kentucky's average was only about $20,000. Kentucky also trails the other states in education. As of 1990, one-third of adult Kentuckians hadn't finished high school. Only Alabama had a smaller number.

In 1990, Kentucky formed a plan to improve its schools. It is called the Kentucky Education Reform Act of 1990. It should be fully in place by 1996. Preschool classes are a major part of the plan. So are family service centers. A good education helps people earn a better living. The new school plan will help improve Kentuckians' lives.

Strip mining (above) and car manufacturing (below) are important Kentucky industries.

Kentuckians and Their Work

KENTUCKIANS AND THEIR WORK

The United States Census counted 3,685,296 Kentuckians in 1990. Of every 100 Kentuckians, 92 are white and 7 are black. Most white Kentuckians have English, Irish, Scottish, or German backgrounds. Other Kentuckians have American Indian, Hispanic, or Asian roots.

About one-half of Kentuckians live in rural areas. They live in small towns or out in the country. Only one-fourth of all other Americans live in rural areas.

Kentucky's country people helped create country music. Some of the best country music stars have come from Kentucky. They include Red Foley and Loretta Lynn. Kentucky was the birthplace of a special kind of country music. It is called bluegrass music. Kentuckian Bill Monroe is called the "Father of Bluegrass Music."

THEIR WORK

One and a half million Kentuckians have jobs. Selling goods is the state's most common type of service work. About 350,000 Kentuckians sell

Above: A Kentucky quilter
Below: A worker at an Oktoberfest food stand

Thoroughbred horses are put through training exercises in a Lexington facility.

A family hikes across a wooden bridge.

goods ranging from food to cars. Kentucky Fried Chicken (KFC) has its headquarters in Louisville. Another popular restaurant chain is Long John Silver's. It is based in Lexington.

The state has more than 380,000 other service workers. They include nurses, doctors, lawyers, and hotel workers. The Frontier Nursing Service has its headquarters in Wendover. It provides nursing care in the Appalachian countryside. The Humana hospital chain is headquartered in Louisville.

About 300,000 Kentuckians make products. Cars, trucks, and parts for them are the state's leading products. Nine-tenths of the bourbon whiskey made in America comes from Kentucky. Meats and baked goods are leading foods. Other Kentucky-made goods include chemicals, cigarettes, and machinery.

Kentucky has more than 250,000 government workers. They include teachers and military people. Fort Knox and Fort Campbell are army bases in the state.

Kentucky has about 93,000 farms. Only Texas, Missouri, and Iowa have more. Raising Thoroughbred horses and beef cattle is Kentucky's leading kind of farm work. Milk, eggs, chickens, and hogs are other livestock products. Tobacco is

Kentucky's leading crop. Only North Carolina tops Kentucky at growing tobacco. Corn, soybeans, and wheat are other major Kentucky crops.

Kentucky is home to about 35,000 miners. Coal is the state's top mining product. Kentucky, Wyoming, and West Virginia are tied as the leading coal-mining states. Oil, natural gas, and limestone are also mined in Kentucky.

Some Kentuckians are tobacco farmers (left) or strip miners (right).

Overleaf: The Levi Jackson Mill at Levi Jackson Wilderness Road State Park

31

A Trip Through the Bluegrass State

A Trip Through the Bluegrass State

K entucky has many interesting places to visit. The state has Abraham Lincoln's birthplace. Kentucky has one of the world's most famous caves. A moonbow appears over one of the state's waterfalls.

Kentucky's Western Third

Wickliffe is in far western Kentucky. It is a good place to start a tour of the state. After a 1,000-mile journey, the Ohio River empties into the Mississippi there. About 1,000 years ago, Indians had a town where Wickliffe now stands. The Wickliffe Mounds Museum has tools from these ancient people.

Paducah is a short way up the Ohio River from Wickliffe. It is an important port on the river. Explorer William Clark laid out Paducah in 1827. The Alben W. Barkley Museum in Paducah honors a famous Kentuckian. Barkley worked as a lawyer in Paducah before becoming vice-president. The Museum of the American Quilter's Society opened in Paducah in 1990. It shows that quilts are works of art.

Whitehaven, in Paducah, is the State of Kentucky Welcome Center.

To the southeast is Murray. It is home to Murray State University. The National Boy Scouting Museum is at this school. Kentuckian Daniel Beard was a main founder of the Boy Scouts of America.

A large vacationland is just east of Murray. It includes two big artificially made lakes and the land between them. The lakes are Kentucky Lake and Lake Barkley. The land in between is the Land Between the Lakes National Recreation Area. This is home to a buffalo herd. People also visit the area to hike, enjoy water sports, and bird-watch.

On the Ohio River in western Kentucky is Henderson. John James Audubon spent about ten

Left: Canoers at Land Between the Lakes Right: John James Audubon painted this Kentucky warbler when he lived in Henderson.

Lake Barkley was named for Vice-President Alben W. Barkley.

35

years there. He explored the woods. He drew pictures of birds he saw. Audubon State Park is on land the artist once roamed. His paintings can be seen at the park's Audubon State Museum.

Owensboro is a short way up the Ohio River from Henderson. The town was settled about 1800. Today, Owensboro is the state's third-largest city. Owensboro is one of the business and arts centers of western Kentucky. Visitors stop at its natural-science and fine-arts museums.

Fairview lies south of Owensboro near the Tennessee border. Jefferson Davis was born there. A 351-foot-tall monument to Davis stands at his birthplace. Visitors can view Kentucky's countryside from the top of this 35-story tower.

MID-KENTUCKY

Robert and George Moore settled along the Barren River in 1780. The brothers played a game called "bowling on the green." The town they helped found was named Bowling Green. Bowling Green is the state's fifth-largest city. The Kentucky Museum at Bowling Green has displays on Kentucky history.

Mammoth Cave is a short drive northeast from Bowling Green. *Mammoth* means "big." Mammoth

Mammoth Cave

Cave is part of the world's longest known cave system. The underground passages extend for more than 330 miles. At Christmastime, Mammoth Cave hosts the Christmas Sing. People come to hear Christmas carols. The singing echoes through the cave.

Abraham Lincoln's birthplace is northeast of Mammoth Cave. The log cabin can be seen near Hodgenville. Lincoln's family moved about 10 miles away when he was two. At Knob Creek stands a cabin like Lincoln's second home.

Bardstown is north of Knob Creek. In 1852, Stephen Foster, a great songwriter, is said to have

The cabin where Abraham Lincoln was born is protected inside this building at Abraham Lincoln's Birthplace National Park near Hodgenville.

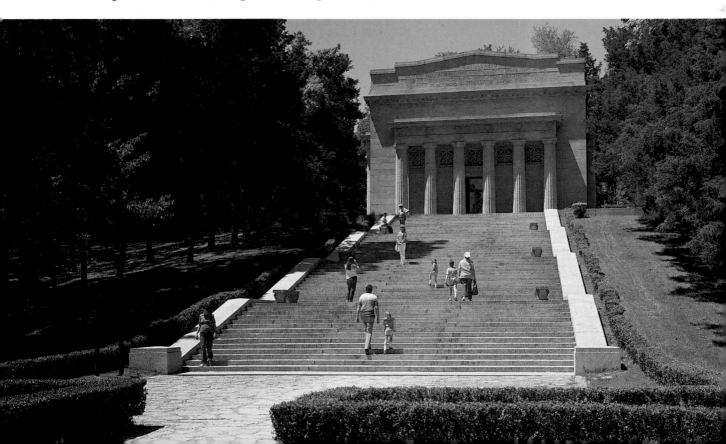

Louisville scenes

My Old Kentucky Home State Park

visited relatives there. Their home inspired him to write "My Old Kentucky Home." This mansion is now called "My Old Kentucky Home."

Fort Knox is west of Bardstown. The United States Gold Depository is there. About $6 billion worth of gold is stored in this building. Tourists are not allowed to enter the building. But they may view it from Gold Vault Road.

Louisville lies on the Ohio River north of Fort Knox. Revolutionary War hero George Rogers Clark helped found the town in 1778. He was the older brother of William Clark, the founder of Paducah. Louisville was named for Louis XVI, the king of France. He had helped the Americans win their freedom from England.

Today, Louisville is Kentucky's largest city. It is also Kentucky's banking and business center. Cigarettes, whiskey, and chemicals come from Louisville. Baseball bats called "Louisville Sluggers" are made nearby. The world's largest publisher of books for blind people is in Louisville. The American Printing House for the Blind offers tours.

The American Printing House for the Blind prints books in Braille. Braille letters are made of raised dots that blind people can read by touching them.

Each year since 1875, Louisville has hosted the Kentucky Derby. The race is called the "Run for the Roses." Besides money, the winning horse earns a blanket of roses. The crowd sings "My Old Kentucky Home" before the race starts. The

Horses racing in the Kentucky Derby

A football game between the University of Kentucky Wildcats and the University of Tennessee Volunteers

Kentucky Derby Museum at Churchill Downs tells the Kentucky Derby story.

Each summer, Louisville hosts the Kentucky State Fair. Kentuckians display their farm products and crafts at the fair.

Louisville has a famous art museum. This is the J. B. Speed Art Museum. It has works by Rembrandt and Picasso. The Museum of History and Science has displays on caves and space travel. The University of Louisville sports teams are the Cardinals. The 1980 and 1986 basketball teams were national college champions.

Kentucky's second-largest city is east of Louisville. This is Lexington. The town was laid out in 1779. It was named for the Massachusetts town where the Revolutionary War began. Mary Todd Lincoln was born in Lexington. She was the wife of President Abraham Lincoln. Her girlhood home is open to visitors. Kentucky's oldest college, Transylvania, is in Lexington. The city is also home to the University of Kentucky.

Lexington is in the heart of the Kentucky Bluegrass. The city is called the "Horse Capital of the World." Horse farms surround the city. Some of them offer tours. Lexington's horse farms are famous for raising Thoroughbreds. These horses

were first bred in Europe 300 years ago. They are used for racing. During the 1800s, Lexington horse farms started breeding the American Saddle Horse. This is a high-stepping horse. It is used for horse shows and pleasure riding. The Kentucky Horse Park is in Lexington. Visitors can see more than forty breeds of horses there.

Shaker Village at Pleasant Hill is south of Lexington. It was founded in 1809. It was one of nineteen Shaker communities in the United States. The Shakers were a religious group. They believed in a simple life filled with peace and love. The Shakers invented the clothespin and the flat broom.

Visitors to Shaker Village at Pleasant Hill can watch craftspeople demonstrate such crafts as broom making and yarn spinning.

The Shakers were named for their habit of shaking during worship.

41

Frankfort is west of Lexington. This city was founded in 1786. Frankfort has been Kentucky's capital since 1793. Kentucky's lawmakers meet in the capitol building. The Floral Clock is behind the capitol. The face of this huge clock is made of thousands of flowers.

The Kentucky Vietnam Veterans Memorial is also in Frankfort. It has the names of more than 1,000 Kentuckians who were killed in Vietnam. A giant sundial is part of the memorial. The sundial's shadow touches each name on the date of the person's death.

The Kentucky Military History Museum and the Kentucky State Historical Museum are also in Frankfort. Both are operated by the Kentucky Historical Society.

Exterior and interior views of the Kentucky State Capitol, in Frankfort

Covington is in Kentucky's northern tip. The town was begun in 1815. It was named for General Leonard Covington. He was an American war hero. Today, Covington is Kentucky's fourth-largest city. Covington lies across the Ohio River from Cincinnati, Ohio. The John A. Roebling Bridge links the two cities.

The Basilica of the Assumption is in Covington. This church has one of the world's largest stained-glass windows. Covington also has one of the country's few animated clocks. It is at the Carroll Chimes Bell Tower. The clock's twenty-one little figures march out every hour. They perform the story of "The Pied Piper of Hamelin."

EASTERN KENTUCKY

Eastern Kentucky has mountains, woods, coal mines, and small farms. The mountain people call their narrow valleys "hollows" or "hollers."

Ashland is eastern Kentucky's largest city. It lies along the Ohio River in far northeastern Kentucky. Ashland is an oil-refining and steel-making center. The Kentucky Highlands Museum is in Ashland. It has displays on Jean Thomas and Jesse Stuart. Thomas traveled through the mountains collecting

Traipse *is an old word meaning "to travel around."*

Yahoo Falls is Kentucky's highest waterfall.

folk songs. People called her the "Traipsin' Woman." Stuart was a schoolteacher. He became an author. Stuart wrote about Kentucky's mountain people.

Eastern Kentucky's mountain people are famous for crafts and country music. Berea is Kentucky's "Crafts Capital." It is south of Lexington. Berea College is there. It keeps Kentucky's old-time crafts alive. Besides the usual courses, Berea College offers many crafts classes. Making baskets, pottery, and dolls are a few of them.

Renfro Valley is near Berea. It is called Kentucky's "Country Music Capital." On Saturday nights, barn dances are held in this town.

Blue Heron Coal Camp is in southeast Kentucky. It operated from 1937 to 1962. Visitors get there by a 6-mile train trip through rugged hills. They can explore the old town and enter the mine. People who once lived there have made recordings. They bring the old coal town to life.

Eastern Kentucky also has many scenic spots. Near the Blue Heron Coal Camp is Yahoo Falls. It has a 113-foot drop. That makes it the state's highest waterfall. Cumberland Falls is nearby. A moonbow can be seen at this waterfall. This happens on clear nights when the moon is full. This rare event is

like a rainbow. But the moon and not the sun is the light source. Cumberland Falls is North America's only waterfall that makes a moonbow.

Eastern Kentucky has many reminders of Daniel Boone. Daniel Boone National Forest takes up much of the land. Barbourville holds the Daniel Boone Festival each October. People dress in pioneer clothes. They enjoy music and games dating back to Boone's time. The trail Boone blazed is now part of Cumberland Gap National Historic Park. The park is in the far southeastern tip of Kentucky.

Cumberland Falls (above) sometimes makes a moonbow. It is created when moonlight strikes drops of water.

A Gallery of Famous Kentuckians

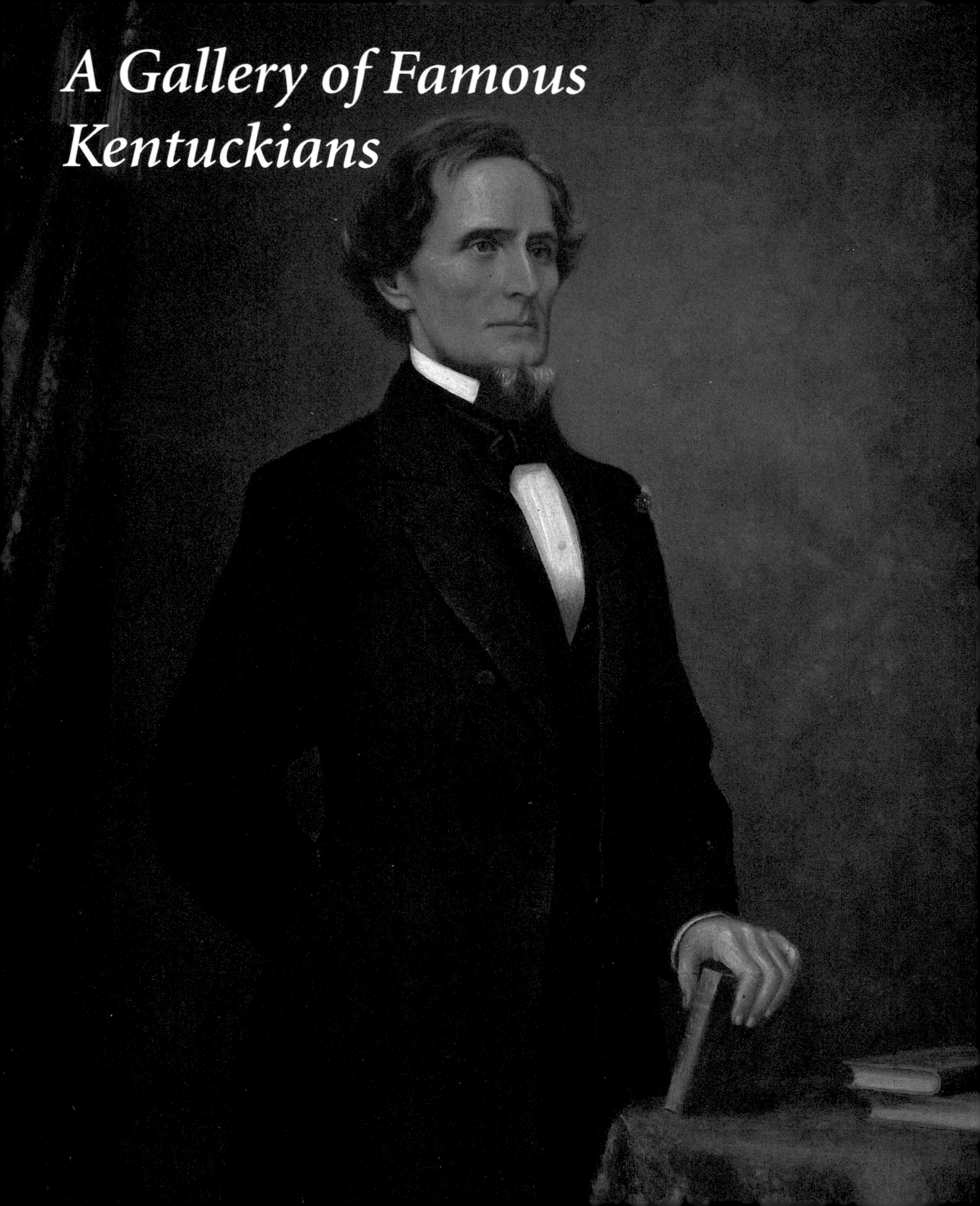

A GALLERY OF FAMOUS KENTUCKIANS

Many Kentuckians have left their marks on the world. They include authors, athletes, and a fried-chicken king.

Daniel Boone (1734-1820) was born in Pennsylvania. He settled Boonesboro in 1775. In 1778, Shawnee Indians captured Boone. He later escaped and hiked 160 miles to Boonesboro. He saved it from an Indian attack. Boone County and Booneville, Kentucky, were named for him.

Henry Clay (1777-1852) was born in Virginia. He later became a Kentucky lawmaker. He tried to settle the country's disputes over slavery. People called him the "Great Compromiser." He coined the famous saying: "I had rather be right than be president."

Zachary Taylor (1784-1850) was born in Virginia but grew up in Louisville. He served in three wars: the War of 1812, the Black Hawk War, and the Mexican War. That's how he got the nickname "Old Rough and Ready." He was the twelfth president of the United States (1849-1850).

Jefferson Davis (1808-1889) was born near Fairview. He married President Taylor's daughter

Daniel Boone

Opposite: Jefferson Davis

47

John C. Breckinridge

Alben Barkley

Sarah. Davis was president of the Confederacy (1861-1865). Before that, he served as U.S. secretary of war (1853-1857) for President Pierce.

Abraham Lincoln (1809-1865) was born near Hodgenville. That's about 100 miles from Jefferson Davis's birthplace. Lincoln lived in Kentucky for his first seven years. He became a lawyer in Illinois and served in Congress (1847-1849). In 1861, he became the sixteenth president of the United States. Through his work, the Union was saved during the Civil War. Five days after the war ended, Lincoln was shot to death.

Kentucky has also produced four vice-presidents. Three of them held office during the 1800s. They were **Richard M. Johnson** (1781-1850) of

Scott County, **John Cabell Breckinridge** (1821-1875) of Lexington, and **Adlai E. Stevenson** (1835-1914) of Christian County. **Alben W. Barkley** (1877-1956) of Paducah worked for FDR's New Deal as a U.S. senator. He then served as vice-president (1949-1953) under President Harry Truman.

The U.S. Supreme Court is the country's highest court. Eight Supreme Court judges were born in Kentucky. One of them, **Louis Brandeis** (1856-1941), was born in Louisville. He became a lawyer. Brandeis was called "the people's attorney." He often took cases without being paid. In 1916, Brandeis became the first Jewish person on the Supreme Court.

Fred Vinson (1890-1953) was born in Louisa. He was another Kentuckian who was named to the Supreme Court. Vinson had a strange start for a judge. He was born in a jail. His father was the town jailer. The family lived in the jail building. Vinson was U.S. secretary of the treasury from 1945 to 1946. He became chief justice of the Supreme Court in 1946.

Albert B. "Happy" Chandler (1898-1991) was born in Corydon. He was Kentucky's governor (1935-1939, 1955-1959) and a U.S. Senator

Adlai E. Stevenson I

Louis Brandeis

For my friend Col R. T. Durrett —
Enid Yandell.

Right: Sculptor Enid Yandell with her statue of Daniel Boone
Below: Martha Layne Collins

(1939-1945). Chandler is best known as the commissioner of baseball (1945-1951). In 1982, he was elected to the Baseball Hall of Fame.

Kentucky's first woman governor was **Martha Layne Collins** (1983-1987). She was born in Shelby County in 1936. She went to the University of Kentucky. There, she was Queen of the Kentucky Derby Festival. Before entering politics, Collins taught school. As governor, she worked for better schools.

Enid Yandell (1870-1934) was born in Louisville. She became a gifted sculptor. Her statue of Daniel Boone stands in Louisville's Cherokee Park.

Cora Wilson Stewart (1875-1958) was born in Powell County. As a child, she had a school for neighborhood children in her yard. In 1911, she started night schools for adults. They were called "moonlight schools." More than 130,000 Kentuckians learned to read at these schools.

Mary Breckinridge (1881-1965) was born in Tennessee. She was Vice-President John C. Breckinridge's granddaughter. After her daughter and son died, she helped other people's children. In 1925, Breckinridge founded Kentucky's Frontier Nursing Service (FNS). She brought health care to people in hard-to-reach mountain areas. People paid for care with eggs, chickens, and vegetables.

Garrett Morgan (1877-1963) was born in Paris, Kentucky. He helped invent the traffic light. This great black inventor also created a gas mask. Morgan once wore it to save men trapped by a tunnel explosion.

Colonel Harland Sanders (1890-1980) was born in Indiana. Later, he ran a restaurant in Corbin. It served fried chicken that was very tasty.

Mary Breckinridge

Garrett Morgan

Loretta Lynn at the Grand Ole Opry

Sanders began a chain called Kentucky Fried Chicken (KFC). The Colonel's picture can be seen on KFC signs and boxes.

Author **Robert Penn Warren** (1905-1989) was born in Guthrie. He wrote novels and poems. Warren won the 1947 Pulitzer Prize for fiction for *All the King's Men*. He also won two Pulitzer Prizes for poetry, one in 1958 and another in 1979. Warren was the first U.S. poet laureate (1986).

Kentucky was home to many famous black athletes. **Isaac Murphy** (1856-1896) was born near Lexington. Murphy was the first jockey to win the Kentucky Derby three times (1884, 1890, 1891).

Cassius Clay was born in Louisville in 1942. In 1964, he won the heavyweight title. He then changed his name to **Muhammad Ali.** Ali won the title three more times.

Loretta Lynn was born in Butcher Holler in 1935. She became a famous country singer and composer. Lynn's father was a coal miner. Her most famous song was "Coal Miner's Daughter." It tells of Lynn's pride in her poor but hard-working Kentucky family.

Many famous Kentuckians were horses. One of them was **Man O' War** (1917-1947). He was born near Lexington. Man O' War was a great Thoroughbred. He set world records. He won every race but one.

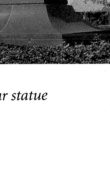

Man O'War statue

The birthplace of Loretta Lynn, Abraham Lincoln, Jefferson Davis, Cora Wilson Stewart, and Muhammad Ali . . .

Home also to Daniel Boone, Mary Breckinridge, and Colonel Harland Sanders . . .

Site of the Kentucky Derby, Mammoth Cave, and the U.S. Gold Depository at Fort Knox . . .

Today, a great producer of coal, tobacco, and racehorses . . .

This is Kentucky—the Bluegrass State!

Did You Know?

One day, a twelve-year-old Louisville boy had his new bike stolen. He told a policeman at a nearby gym. The policeman couldn't find the bike, but he convinced the boy to join his boxing class. This was how Cassius Clay (later Muhammad Ali) got his start in boxing.

Long ago, some Kentucky men had the first name "Green." Green Murphy was jockey Isaac Murphy's grandfather.

Kentucky produced the youngest and oldest vice-presidents. John C. Breckinridge was just thirty-six when he became vice-president. Alben W. Barkley was seventy-five when he left office.

Daniel Beard grew up in Covington. He founded the Sons of Daniel Boone, a forerunner of the Boy Scouts. Later, he headed the Boy Scouts of America for thirty-one years. Alaska's Mount Beard was named for "Uncle Dan," as Scouts called him.

Families that argue are often said to be just like the Hatfields and the McCoys. The Hatfields were a West Virginia family. The McCoys lived across the border in Pike County, Kentucky. The families fought for many years, resulting in many deaths.

Patrick Henry once owned the land where the Kentucky Horse Park stands. He was the famous Virginian who said: "Give me liberty or give me death!"

Black jockeys won fifteen of the first twenty-eight Kentucky Derbies. Oliver Lewis won the first Derby (1875) aboard Aristides. Alonzo Clayton (1892) and James "Soup" Perkins (1895) were the youngest winning jockeys in Derby history. They were only fifteen.

"Happy Birthday" is one of the world's most popular songs. Louisville teachers Mildred and Patty Hill, who were sisters, wrote this song in 1893.

Kentucky has cities named Dwarf, Eighty-Eight, Halfway, Index, Mousie, Paint Lick, Quicksand, Science Hill, and Stay.

Other communities include Bug, Tiny Town, and Rabbit Hash. But the prize for the strangest name must go to Monkeys Eyebrow.

KENTUCKY INFORMATION

State flag

Goldenrod

Area: 40,395 square miles (the thirty-seventh biggest state)

Greatest Distance North to South: 182 miles

Greatest Distance East to West: 417 miles

Border States: Ohio, Indiana, and Illinois to the north; Missouri to the west; Tennessee to the south; Virginia and West Virginia to the east

Highest Point: Black Mountain, 4,145 feet above sea level

Lowest Point: 257 feet above sea level, along the Mississippi River

Hottest Recorded Temperature: 114° F. (at Greensburg, on July 28, 1930)

Coldest Recorded Temperature: -34° F. (at Cynthiana, on January 28, 1963)

Statehood: The fifteenth state, on June 1, 1792

Origin of Name: Kentucky comes from the Cherokee Indian word *Ken-tah-teh,* which might mean "lands where we will live" or "meadowland"

Capital: Frankfort (since 1793)

Previous Capital: Lexington

Counties: 120

United States Representatives: 6 (as of 1992)

State Senators: 38

State Representatives: 100

State Song: "My Old Kentucky Home" by Stephen Foster

State Motto: "United We Stand, Divided We Fall"

Nickname: "Bluegrass State"

State Seal: Adopted in 1792

State Flag: Adopted in 1918

State Flower: Goldenrod

State Bird: Kentucky Cardinal

State Tree: Kentucky coffeetree

State Animal: Gray squirrel

State Fish: Kentucky bass

Some Rivers: Ohio, Mississippi, Kentucky, Tennessee, Cumberland, Salt, Licking, Rough, Green, Barren, Big Sandy

Some Lakes: Kentucky, Barkley, Dale Hollow, Cumberland, Nolin, Rough River, Green River, Barren River

Some Caves: Mammoth Cave, Crystal Onyx Cave, Jesse James Cave, Carter Caves

Wildlife: Deer, bobcats, raccoons, foxes, squirrels, opossums, rabbits, woodchucks, bats, Kentucky cardinals, woodpeckers, ducks, geese, herons, egrets, many other kinds of birds, many kinds of snakes and turtles, bass, crappies, catfish, many other kinds of fish

Manufactured Products: Cars, trucks, other motor vehicles, parts for motor vehicles, construction equipment and other machinery, baked goods, meats, bourbon whiskey and other drinks, paints, chemicals, cigarettes, air conditioning and heating equipment

Farm Products: Horses and ponies, beef cattle, chickens, hogs, milk, eggs, tobacco, soybeans, wheat, corn for livestock and for popcorn, apples, peaches

Mining Products: Coal, oil, natural gas, limestone

Population: 3,685,296, twenty-third among the fifty states (1990 U.S. Census Bureau figures)

Major Cities (1990 Census):

Louisville	269,063	Hopkinsville	29,809
Lexington	225,366	Paducah	27,256
Owensboro	53,549	Frankfort	25,968
Covington	43,264	Henderson	25,945
Bowling Green	40,641	Ashland	23,622

Kentucky cardinal

Coffeetree

Gray squirrel

Kentucky History

13,000 B.C.—Ancient Indians reach Kentucky

1654—Abraham Wood sends explorers to Kentucky

1673—Gabriel Arthur, another English explorer, enters the region

1750—Thomas Walker discovers the Cumberland Gap

1774—James Harrod establishes Harrodsburg, Kentucky's first non-Indian town

1775—Daniel Boone blazes the Wilderness Road through the Cumberland Gap and founds Boonesboro

1775-83—The United States fights the Revolutionary War and wins its freedom from England

1776-82—George Rogers Clark defends Kentucky settlers from Indian attacks

1778—Louisville is founded

1779—Lexington is founded

1780—Transylvania University is begun in Lexington

1786—Frankfort is founded

1792—Kentucky becomes the fifteenth state on June 1

1793—Frankfort becomes the state capital

1808—Jefferson Davis is born near Fairview on June 3

1809—Abraham Lincoln is born near Hodgenville on February 12

1818—Andrew Jackson helps the United States make the Jackson Purchase from the Chickasaw Indians

1848—Zachary Taylor is elected the twelfth president of the United States

1860—Abraham Lincoln is elected the sixteenth president of the United States

1861—The Civil War begins; Abraham Lincoln leads the Union and Jefferson Davis leads the Confederacy

1862—The Battles of Mill Springs, Richmond, and Perryville are fought in Kentucky

Covington's Market and Square in the 1850s

1865—The Union victory in the Civil War ends slavery

1875—The first Kentucky Derby is run

1891—Kentucky's present constitution is adopted

1904-09—The Black Patch War takes place in western Kentucky between tobacco farmers and tobacco companies

1909—The capitol is completed in Frankfort

1917-18—After the United States enters World War I, about 80,000 Kentuckians help win it

1929-39—Farmers, miners, and other workers suffer during the Great Depression

1936—The United States completes the Gold Depository at Fort Knox

1941—Mammoth Cave National Park is created

1941-45—Once the United States enters World War II, about 325,000 Kentucky men and women help win it

1955—Kentucky lowers its voting age to eighteen

1966—Kentucky adopts a state Civil Rights Act

1977—The U.S. Congress passes a law to limit damage from strip mining

1983—Martha Layne Collins becomes Kentucky's first woman governor

1988—The Toyota Motor Company opens an automobile plant in Georgetown

1990—Kentucky begins a school improvement project; the state's population reaches 3,698,969

1992—Happy 200th birthday, beautiful Bluegrass State!

Abraham Lincoln delivering the Gettysburg Address

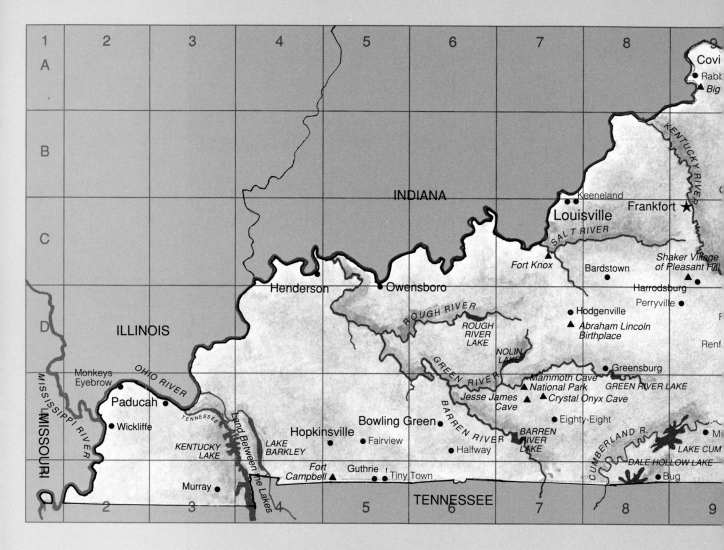

MAP KEY

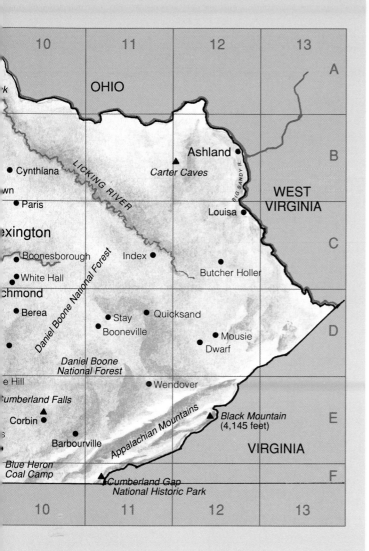

GLOSSARY

ancient: Relating to a time early in history

antislavery: Against slavery

billion: A thousand million (1,000,000,000)

bluegrass: Grass with bluish-green leaves; also a kind of country music

capital: A city that is the seat of government

capitol: A building in which the government meets

civil rights: The rights of a citizen

climate: The typical weather of a region

compromise: To come to an agreement by each side giving in somewhat

depository: A place where something is kept until needed

explorer: A person who visits and studies unknown lands

integration: The process of bringing people of various races together

mammoth (mastodon): A prehistoric animal that was much like an elephant; big, as in Mammoth Cave

manufacturing: The making of products

61

memorial: A building or statue built in memory of a person

million: A thousand thousand (1,000,000)

moonbow: An event like a rainbow, only with the moon and not the sun as the light source

pioneer: A person who is among the first to move into a region

population: The number of people in a place

sculptor: An artist who makes statues and other three-dimensional artworks

segregation: The process of keeping people apart, often based on race

slavery: A practice in which some people are owned by other people

swamp: Wet, spongy land that is sometimes covered by water

tourism: The business of providing services such as food and lodging for travelers

PICTURE ACKNOWLEDGMENTS

Front cover, © W. J. Scott/H. Armstrong Roberts; 1, © Charlie Borland-WildVision; 2, Tom Dunnington; 3 © SuperStock; 4-5, Tom Dunnington; 6-7, © Tom Till/Photographer; 8, © Don Ament; 9 (top), Courtesy of Hammond, Incorporated, Maplewood, New Jersey; 10 (both pictures), © Don Ament; 11 (top left and bottom), © Don Ament; 11 (top right), © Westerman; 12 (left), © Brian Parker/Tom Stack & Associates; 12 (right), © Charlie Westerman; 13 (top), © Barbara L. Moore/N E Stock Photo; 13 (bottom), © Don Ament; 14, © W. J. Scott/H. Armstrong Roberts; 15, National Museum of Natural History/Smithsonian Institution, photo by Charles H. Phillips; 16, © Tom Till/Photographer; 17 (both pictures), © SuperStock; 18, © W. J. Scott/H. Armstrong Roberts; 19 (top), North Wind Picture Archives, hand-colored; 19 (bottom), © Jim Schwabel/N E Stock Photo; 20, Historical Pictures/Stock Montage, Inc.; 21, © Tim Till/Photographer; 22, © Eric Futran Photography; 23,© Richard Nugent; 24, © Don & Pat Valenti/Tony Stone Worldwide/Chicago, Ltd.; 25 (both pictures), AP/Wide World Photos; 26, © Jim Schwabel/N E Stock Photo; 27 (top), © Charlie Westerman; 27 (bottom), © Richard Nugent; 28, © Eric Futran Photography; 29 (top), © Tom McCarthy/Photo Edit; 29 (bottom), © Jeff Friedman/Tony Stone Worldwide/Chicago, Ltd.; 30 (top), © Don Ament; 30 (bottom), © Joan Dunlop; 31 (left), © Eric Futran Photography; 31 (right), © Charlie Westerman; 32-33, © Tom Till/Photographer; 34, © W. J. Scott/H. Armstrong Roberts; 35 (left), © Jerry Hennen; 35 (right), Douglas Kenyon, Inc.; 36, © Richard L. Capps/R/C Photo Agency; 37, © SuperStock; 38 (top left), © Chip & Rosa Maria Peterson; 38 (top right), © SuperStock; 38 (bottom), © W. J. Scott/H. Armstrong Roberts; 39, © Richard Nugent; 40, © Jerry Wachter/Photri, Inc.; 41 (left), © Diane Graham-Henry/Tony Stone Worldwide/Chicago, Ltd.; 41 (right), © Jim Schwabel/N E Stock Photo; 42 (left), © W. J. Scott/H. Armstrong Roberts; 42 (right), © Doris De Witt/ Tony Stone Worldwide/Chicago, Ltd.; 44, © Charlie Borland-WildVision; 45, © Jerry Hennen; 46, The Museum of the Confederacy, Richmond, Virginia, photography by Katherine Wetzel; 47, North Wind Picture Archives, hand-colored; 48 (top), Historical Pictures/Stock Montage, Inc.; 48 (bottom), AP/Wide World Photos; 49 (both pictures), AP/Wide World Photos; 50 (top), The Filson Club; 50 (bottom), AP/Wide World Photos; 51 (both pictures), AP/Wide World Photos; 52, © Donnie Beauchamp; 53, © James P. Rowan/MGA/Photri, Inc.; 54, AP/Wide World Photos; 55 (both pictures), AP/Wide World Photos; 56 (top), Courtesy Flag Research Center, Winchester, Massachusetts 01890; 56 (bottom), © Rod Planck/Tom Stack & Associates; 57 (top), © Mack & Betty Kelley; 57 (middle), © Kitty Kohout/Root Resources; 57 (bottom), © Leonard Lee Rue III/Tom Stack & Associates; 58, North Wind Picture Archives, hand-colored; 59, North Wind Picture Archives, hand-colored; 60-61, Tom Dunnington; back cover: © Tom Till/Photographer